ILLINOIS CENTRAL RAILROAD
1854 THROUGH 1960
PHOTO ARCHIVE

Kim D. Tschudy

D1604894

Iconografix
Photo Archive Series

Iconografix
PO Box 446
Hudson, Wisconsin 54016 USA

Library of Congress Card Number: 2001135743

ISBN 1-58388-063-1

02 03 04 05 06 07 08 5 4 3 2 1

Printed in China

Cover and book design by Shawn Glidden

Copyediting by Suzie Helberg

COVER PHOTO: See page 8.

BOOK PROPOSALS

Iconografix is a publishing company specializing in books for transportation enthusiasts. We publish in a number of different areas, including Automobiles, Auto Racing, Buses, Construction Equipment, Emergency Equipment, Farming Equipment, Railroads & Trucks. The Iconografix imprint is constantly growing and expanding into new subject areas.

Authors, editors, and knowledgeable enthusiasts in the field of transportation history are invited to contact the Editorial Department at Iconografix, Inc., PO Box 446, Hudson, WI 54016.

DEDICATION

This book on the Illinois Central Railroad was a bittersweet project to bring to completion. My memories of the Illinois Central go back to the very early 1950s when my grandfather and I would go off on our jaunts. Quite often those jaunts meant walking through the 1260-foot Stewart Tunnel located four miles from our home. Eventually it fell upon my shoulders to take my sons, Terry and Todd, through the tunnel.

My contract to complete this book arrived in the mail on April 20, 2001. Two years earlier on April 20, 1999, the Green County, Wisconsin, County Board voted 22-6 to rip out and sell for scrap the Illinois Central rails that had served us well for over a century.

I felt a profound sadness that our history could be removed by the foot and sold by the pound to the highest bidder. Just 11 months earlier I visited the Illinois Central's Wallace Yard in Freeport, Illinois. The yardmaster gave me permission to walk back to the switch that in past years routed trains north to Dodgeville and Madison, Wisconsin.

On that warm May morning I pondered what must have gone through the minds of the black people of the south as they migrated north in search of a better life after the Civil War, WWI and WWII. Their trip north on the Illinois Central was one of uncertainty to an unknown land. A land that held the hope of a better life than they had in the south of that time. For them there was no turning back. The Illinois Central was their one hope of a better life in the north. For many it was a hope turned into reality.

This year, 2001, marks the 150th Anniversary of the Illinois Central. The Illinois Central will hold onto its identity until the end of 2001. After that the Illinois Central will no longer exist as an American railroad because it is being merged into the Canadian National Railway system.

I dedicate this book first and foremost to my grandfather, Fred Tschudy, who taught me about the Illinois Central. And to my writing mentors, Herbert Kubly and George Vukelich, who both took me under their wings and taught me that writing with emotion was OK. Also Bob Marsh, a friend who's shared many a railroad story with me. And, finally, to "Italian Worker #132." This man died in 1888 while working on the Illinois Central Stewart Tunnel in the town of Exeter, Green County, Wisconsin. He died nameless, put to his eternal rest in the cemetery behind St. James Catholic Church in Dayton, Wisconsin.

Last, but not least, to my friends in Green and Dane Counties (Wisconsin) who fought the good fight to save our Illinois Central. I say thanks for all you did to try to save our history. You were right in the fight but politics ruled the day. We've shared a lot of laughs and far too many tears over this loss of our heritage.

KDT

INTRODUCTION

Clermont, Iowa, Christmas Eve 2001. The streets are quiet and the churches all are dark. Walking past the Union Sunday School I pause to give thought to the Christmas service held here in 1860. I recall a concert held here this past July that told the story of the Boys of Fayette County as they went off to the Civil War in 1861.

On that Christmas Eve not one of the young men in attendance for the church service could have imagined that within six months they would be leaving their homes in the rich Turkey River Valley to make a 55-mile horse and wagon journey to Independence, Iowa. At Independence they would board the Dubuque & Pacific Railroad, which became absorbed into the Illinois Central system. Few would see home for the next four years. Some would never return, their bodies buried at Shiloh and other battlefields in the South.

On this night when much of the world celebrated Christmas the young men no doubt had thoughts of completing the new church down the street come spring. Little did they think they would become volunteers in Company C of the Twelfth Iowa Infantry Regiment, leaving the building of the new church until their return home in the summer of 1865. The different coloration of the brick walls tells where the work ended in 1860 and resumed in 1865.

Little did the boys of Clermont realize on Christmas Eve 1860 that the traveling salesman from Galena, Illinois, who sold them leather and harness, would one day become General U.S. Grant. Nor did they realize that one in attendance, David Henderson, who lost a leg in the war, would become the Speaker of the U.S. House of Representatives.

The Illinois Central Railroad probably did more to win the Civil War than all other railroads combined. Unlike other railroads that oriented their lines on an East-West heading the Illinois Central focused on North-South routes. That decision led the Illinois Central to boast having moved 31% of the troops and 30% of the Civil War material through Cairo, Illinois.

Begun in 1851, the Illinois Central, on their 100th anniversary held the distinction of having never defaulted on a single bond or loan payment. No other American railroad could boast the famous people associated with the railroad. Abraham Lincoln served as the railroad attorney, charging $15 per case handled. Samuel Clemens (Mark Twain) worked for the Illinois Central as a steamboat pilot between 1859-1861. In 1869 Andrew Carnegie built the Dubuque Bridge. After the Civil War the Illinois Central employed a number of Civil War generals.

As the Illinois Central moved south to the Gulf of Mexico it purchased a number of smaller railroads. The South used a narrower gauge than the standard 4-foot 8 1/2-inch gauge used in the north. This required all cars to be changed out when they crossed the river at Cairo.

In July 1881 30,000 railroad workers began at dawn to change the lines south of Cairo, Illinois, to the standard gauge used in the north. By 3 p.m. that same day the job of converting 547 miles of rail from Cairo to New Orleans was complete.

The Illinois Central is immortalized in a pair of very popular songs. Every grade school child in America has no doubt heard the story of the most famous engineer in history, John Luther (Casey) Jones and the wreck he had near Vaughn, Mississippi, in 1900. Steve Goldman's "City of New Orleans" is to railroading what the Edmund Fitzgerald is to Great Lakes shipping.

This book on the Illinois Central is but a tiny glimpse at the railroad that called itself the Mainline of Mid-America. The story of the Illinois Central is the story of the people who call the Midwest home. When news of the coming of the first train to a town arrived, along with it came the hope of economic prosperity and the ability to move people and products to far away places, and the Illinois Central changed hope to reality.

The Illinois Central no longer exists, having been absorbed into the Canadian National Railway system in 2001. However, the memories of the Illinois Central remain forever.

Thanks to the Civil War effort of the Illinois Central, many of the boys of Clermont returned home alive in 1865. Farewell old friend. You've served us well.

Note: Generally, a builder's name and construction number is listed along with the build date. For the most part, the photographs are arranged chronologically from the oldest to newest.

KDT 12/24/01

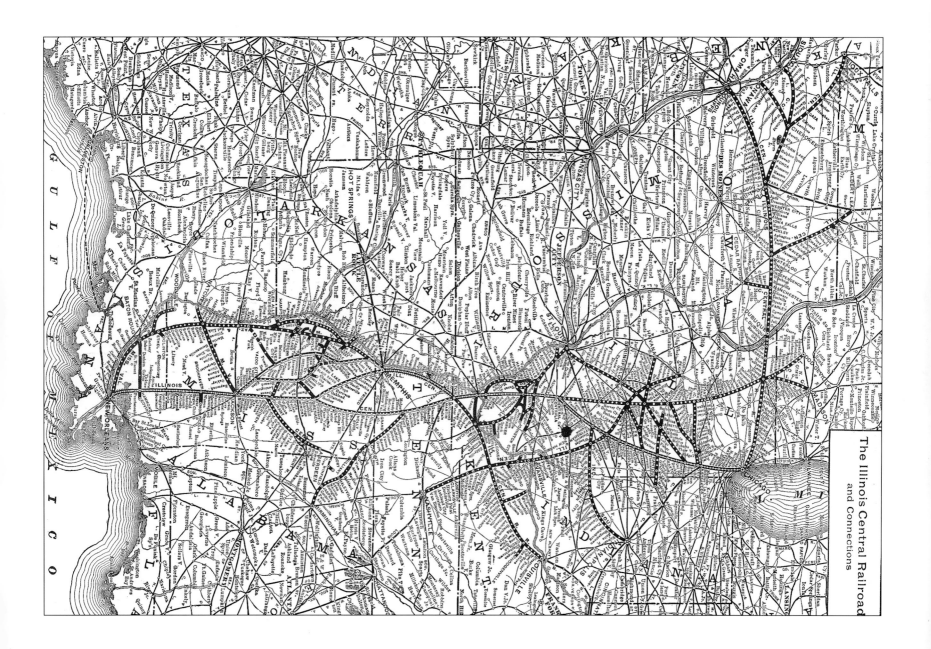

Illinois Central Locomotive #1422 Type 4-4-0 Eight-Wheeler. Locomotive #1422 was built by Rogers Locomotive Works in May 1854 as #492. It was originally numbered #50 and renumbered to #1422 in July 1890. The July 1890 system-wide renumbering was done to bring order to classes of locomotives. This locomotive was acquired with assimilation of smaller railroads into the Illinois Central. It was rebuilt in November 1876 and dropped from the roster between 1890-1896. *Author's Collection.*

Illinois Central Locomotive #1425 Type 4-4-0 Eight-Wheeler. Locomotive #1425 was built by Rogers Locomotive Works in June 1855 as #586. It was originally numbered #69 and was renumbered to #1425 and dropped from the roster between 1896-1898. *Author's Collection.*

Illinois Central Locomotive #95 Type 0-4-0 Four-Wheeler. Locomotive #95 was built by Rogers Locomotive Works as #746 in March 1857 and retired from the roster in December 1883. *Author's Collection.*

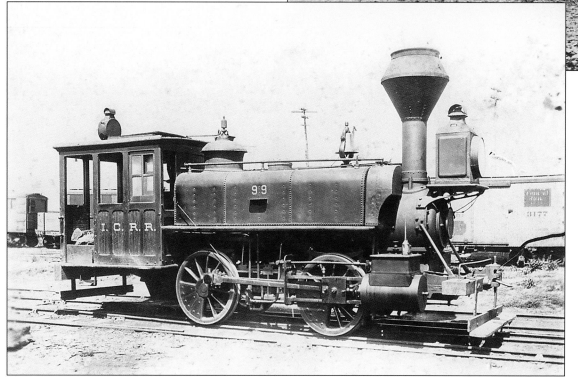

Illinois Central Locomotive #99 Type 0-4-0 Four-Wheeler. Locomotive #99 was built by Grant in June 1873. It was originally built for New Orleans Belt Railroad, sold to CSt.LN&O and numbered as #11. When the IC obtained this locomotive it was renumbered to #257 and in 1890 renumbered to #99 and sold the same year. *Author's Collection.*

Illinois Central Locomotive #201 Type 2-4-4-T Suburban. Photographed at the Chicago Rail Fair on August 29, 1948, it was built by Rogers Locomotive Works as #2588 in May 1880. It was originally numbered as #213, renumbered to #221 in 1884, renumbered again to #201 in July 1890, and renumbered again to #1401 in July 1900. Today #201 resides in Owatonna, Minnesota, where it's on display. *Mike Gruber Collection.*

Illinois Central Locomotive #731 Type 2-6-0 Mogul. Locomotive #731 was built by Illinois Central Shops as #6 in July 1880. It was renumbered as #466 and renumbered again to #731 in 1890, and renumbered to #1731 in May 1903. It was again renumbered to #2731 in January 1915 and was scrapped in February 1916. *Author's Collection.*

Illinois Central Locomotive #1798 Type 2-6-0 Mogul. Locomotive #1798 was built by Baldwin Locomotive Works as #5379 in November 1880. Originally built for the Paducah and Elizabethtown Railroad as #18, it was renumbered to #798 in 1896, renumbered again to #1798 in May 1904 and scrapped in June 1914. *Author's Collection.*

Illinois Central Locomotive #1304 Type 4-4-0 Eight-Wheeler. Locomotive #1304 was built by IC shops in December 1880 and was originally numbered #12. It was renumbered in 1884 to #53, to #1134 in July 1890, and again in 1899 to #1304. It retired from the roster in November 1909. *Author's Collection.*

Illinois Central Locomotive #1402 Type 2-4-4-T Suburban. Locomotive #1402 was built by Rogers Locomotive Works as #2691 in February 1881. It was originally numbered as #214, renumbered to #222 in 1884, renumbered again to #1402 in July 1900, and was then sold to Briggs & Turivas in March 1928. *Author's Collection.*

Illinois Central Locomotive #1436 Type 4-6-0 Ten-Wheeler. Locomotive #1436 was built by Schenectady Locomotive Works as #1608 in October 1881. It was originally numbered as #37 for the Chesapeake, Ohio & Southwestern Railroad and was acquired by the Illinois Central in 1896. At that time it was renumbered to #254, was rebuilt in May 1903, and renumbered to #1436 Suburban. It was sold to Briggs & Turivis in March 1928. *Author's Collection.*

Illinois Central Locomotive #1534 Type 0-4-0 Four-Wheeler. Locomotive #1534 was built by Brooks Locomotive Works as #704 in April 1882. Originally purchased by the Peoria, Decatur & Evansville RR, this locomotive was acquired by the IC in September 1900. It was renumbered to #1534 and later to #2534, then retired from the roster in May 1914. *Author's Collection.*

Illinois Central Locomotive #2510 Type 0-4-0 Four-Wheeler. Locomotive #2510 was built by Illinois Central Shops in September 1882. It was originally numbered as #20, renumbered to #10 in 1890, renumbered again to #1510 in 1898, and renumbered to #2510 in 1912. It was rebuilt in 1917 and retired in June 1935. *Author's Collection.*

Illinois Central Locomotive #1 Type 0-4-0 Four-Wheeler. Locomotive #1 was built by Illinois Central shops in March 1884. Originally numbered as #11 and renumbered to #1 in 1890, renumbered to #1501 in 1898, and renumbered to #2501 in 1912. It was rebuilt and retired in 1914. *Author's Collection.*

Illinois Central Locomotive #2176 Type 4-4-0 Eight-Wheeler. Locomotive #2176 was built by Illinois Central Shops in December 1885. It was originally numbered as #254 and renumbered to #1176 in July 1890, renumbered to #2176 in 1912, and dropped from the roster between 1921 and 1924. *Author's Collection.*

Illinois Central Locomotive #1806 Type 2-6-0 Mogul. Photographed in front of the Basco, Wisconsin, depot, #1806 was built by Alco Brooks Locomotive Works as #1173 in January 1887. It was originally numbered as #359, renumbered in July 1890 to #806, renumbered again in May 1904 to #1806, and was retired in February 1916. This locomotive, along with locomotives 354 through 363, were built for the Chicago, Madison, and Northern branch line from Freeport, Illinois, to Madison, Wisconsin. This last remaining Illinois Central line in Wisconsin was removed in 1999. *Fred Solberger Collection.*

Illinois Central Locomotive #4904 Type 4-4-0 Eight-Wheeler. Locomotive #4904 was built by Illinois Central Shops in June 1888. It was originally numbered as #164 and renumbered to #904 in June 1890, renumbered again in May 1906 to #1904, and renumbered again between 1921 and 1924 to #4904. It was retired from the roster in July 1929. *Author's Collection.*

Illinois Central Locomotive #1910 Type 4-4-0 Eight-Wheeler. Locomotive #1910 was built by Alco Brooks Locomotive Works as #1754 in October 1890. It was originally numbered as #910, renumbered again to #1910 in May 1906, again renumbered to #4910 between 1921 to 1924, and was retired in July 1935. *Author's Collection.*

Illinois Central Locomotive #4905 Type 4-4-0 Eight-Wheeler. Locomotive #4905 was built by Alco Brooks Locomotive Works as #1749 in October 1890. It was originally numbered as #905, renumbered to #1905 in May 1906, and renumbered to #4905 between 1921 and 1924. It was scrapped in June 1940. *Author's Collection.*

Illinois Central Locomotive #232 Type 2-6-4-T Suburban. Locomotive #232 was built by Rogers Locomotive Works as #4798 in December 1892. It was renumbered as #1423 in July 1900, and was sold to a sand and gravel company in Coleman, Illinois, in November 1926. *Author's Collection.*

Illinois Central Locomotive #930 Type 4-4-0 Eight-Wheeler. Locomotive #930 was built by Rogers Locomotive Works as #4695 in May 1892. It was originally numbered as #930, renumbered to #1930, renumbered again to #4930 and retired from the roster in March 1928. *Author's Collection.*

Illinois Central Locomotive #442 Type 2-6-0 Mogul. Locomotive #442 was built by Rogers Locomotive Works as #4921 in September 1893. It was scrapped in 1954. *Author's Collection.*

Illinois Central Locomotive #459 Type 2-6-0 Mogul. Locomotive #459 was built by Rogers Locomotive Works as #5022 in December 1894 and scrapped in October 1938. *Author's Collection.*

Illinois Central Locomotive #473 Type 2-6-0 Mogul. Locomotive #473 was built by Alco Brooks Locomotive Works as #2602 in November 1895 and was scrapped in 1955. Photographed in the scrap line at Paducah, Kentucky, by C. Ulrich in May 1955. The main piston rod is missing so Ulrich inserted an old beer can in place to fake it. Negative is part of C.T. Felstead Collection, owned by William Raia.

Illinois Central Locomotive #484 Type 2-6-0 Mogul. Locomotive #484 was built by Alco Brooks Locomotive Works as #2613 in November 1895 and was scrapped or sold in June 1951. During its life #484 was used to pull a Chicago Railroad and Locomotive Historical Society special train on the Freeport, Illinois, to Dodgeville, Wisconsin, branch-line on October 8, 1939. On June 15, 1941, just one year before this branch was abandoned, the Rockford, Illinois, Movie Makers Club chartered a train to Dodgeville. When the Dodgeville branch was abandoned #484 was transferred to Rantoul, Illinois, and worked Potomac-Leroy branches before being replaced. *Author's Collection.*

This montage of photographs shows Locomotive #484 Type 2-6-0 Mogul pulling the Chicago Locomotive and Railroad Historical Society charter trip on October 8, 1939. These photographs were taken near Hollandale, Wisconsin. *Joe Hendrickson Collection.*

Illinois Central Locomotive #23 Type 4-6-0 Four-Wheeler at Chicago in 1906. Locomotive #23 was built by Alco Brooks Locomotive Works as #3289 in August 1899. Locomotive #23 was sold to the Mexican government in 1921 and renumbered to #859. *Author's Collection.*

Opposite page top. Illinois Central Locomotive #488 Type 2-6-0 Mogul. Photographed in Freeport, Illinois, #488 was built by Alco Brooks Locomotive Works as #2643 in February 1896 and was scrapped in October 1946. This locomotive, along with #484 and #485, were regulars on the Dodgeville, Wisconsin, branch. *Author's Collection.*

Opposite page bottom. Illinois Central Locomotive #491 Type 2-6-0 Mogul. Photographed near West Junction in Freeport, Illinois, in 1898. Locomotive #491 was built by Alco Brooks Locomotive Works as #2646 in March 1896 and was scrapped in November 1945. *Author's Collection.*

Illinois Central Locomotive #181 Type 0-6-0-T Six-Wheeler. Locomotive #181 was built by Alco Brooks Locomotive Works as #3282 in August 1899. At some point in its life it was converted to a 0-6-4-T and scrapped in April 1946. *Author's Collection.*

Illinois Central Locomotive #5022 Type 4-6-0 Ten-Wheeler. Locomotive #5022 was built by Rogers Locomotive Works as #5454 in October 1899. Photographed in Peoria, Illinois, it was originally numbered as #392. It was renumbered to #222 in July 1900. It was renumbered to #2022 in July or August 1907 and again renumbered to #5022 in 1922. It was retired from the roster in June 1935. *Author's Collection.*

Illinois Central Locomotive #552 Type 2-6-0 Mogul. Locomotive #552 was built by Rogers Locomotive Works as #5622 in September 1900. It was retired in October 1938. *Author's Collection.*

Illinois Central Locomotive #192 Type 0-6-0 Switcher. Locomotive #192 was built by Rogers Locomotive Works as #5633 in October 1900. It was scrapped in June 1935. *Author's Collection.*

Illinois Central Locomotive #564 Type 2-6-0 Mogul. Locomotive #564 was built by Alco Brooks Locomotive Works as #3701 in December 1900. It was retired in 1939 and its boiler was installed on Locomotive #563. *Author's Collection.*

Illinois Central Locomotive #359 Type 0-6-0 Six-Wheeler started its life as Illinois Central Locomotive #575, a Type 2-6-0 locomotive. Locomotive #359 was built by Pittsburgh Locomotive Works as #2298 in July 1901. Built as a 2-6-0 Mogul, it was rebuilt to a Type 0-6-0 locomotive in September 1943 and renumbered as #359 at that time (and usually assigned to Asylum, Mississippi, yards after conversion). It was scrapped in October 1946. *Author's Collection.*

Illinois Central Locomotive #572 Type 2-6-0 Mogul. Locomotive #572 was built by Pittsburgh Locomotive Works as #2295 in August 1901, was retired in May 1940, and its boiler was installed on Illinois Central Locomotive #582. *Author's Collection.*

Illinois Central Locomotive #3301 Type 2-8-0 Consolidation. Locomotive #3301 was built by Rogers Locomotive Works as #5877 in January 1903. It was photographed here in Carbondale, Illinois, on September 14, 1937, by R.J. Foster. It was originally numbered as #682 and renumbered to #724 in January 1943. In June 1937 it was rebuilt to 0-8-0 Switcher #3301 and scrapped in 1950. The boiler went to Locomotive #683. *Author's Collection.*

Illinois Central Locomotive #694 Type 2-8-0 Consolidation. Locomotive #694 was built by Alco Schenectady Locomotive Works as #27199 in January 1903. It was scrapped in November 1939. Most of the locomotives in this series were renumbered but #694 carried the same number from the beginning of its service until its end of service with Illinois Central. Locomotives from this number group were converted and renumbered to 3300 class 0-8-0s. Those not chosen were either renumbered into 700 class or scrapped. *Author's Collection.*

Illinois Central Locomotive #1010 Type 4-4-2 Atlantic is shown in this photograph being checked by the engineer readying the locomotive to pull Illinois Central train #129 out of Dixon, Illinois, in 1932. Locomotive #1010 was built by Rogers Locomotive Works as #5939 in April 1903. In 1942 it was renumbered to #2002 and dropped from the roster between 1943 and 1951. This locomotive often worked on passenger and charter trips between Freeport and Clinton, Illinois. *Author's collection.*

Illinois Central Locomotive #719 Type 2-8-0 Consolidation. Locomotive #719 was built by Rogers Locomotive Works as #5988 in July 1903. It was scrapped in 1951. *Author's Collection.*

Illinois Central Locomotive #730 Type 2-8-0 Consolidation. Locomotive #730 was built by Rogers Locomotive Works as #5999 in August 1903. It was scrapped in 1949 and the boiler went to 2-8-0 #706, which was renumbered to #730. *Author's Collection.*

Illinois Central Locomotive #732 Type 2-8-0 Consolidation. Locomotive #732 was built by Rogers Locomotive Works as #6079 in October 1903. It was rebuilt as a Type 0-8-0 Switcher in May 1942 and renumbered to #3317. It was dropped from the roster between 1943 and 1951. *Author's Collection.*

Illinois Central Locomotive #733 Type 2-8-0 Consolidation built by Rogers Locomotive Works as #6080 in October 1903. It was rebuilt in October 1942 as an 0-8-0 and renumbered to #3330. It was scrapped in 1950. *Author's Collection.*

Illinois Central Locomotive #84 Type 0-6-0 Switcher. Locomotive #84 was built by Alco Brooks Locomotive Works as #28019 in January 1904. Photographed in Clinton, Illinois, in 1939, it was dropped from the roster in 1941. *Author's Collection.*

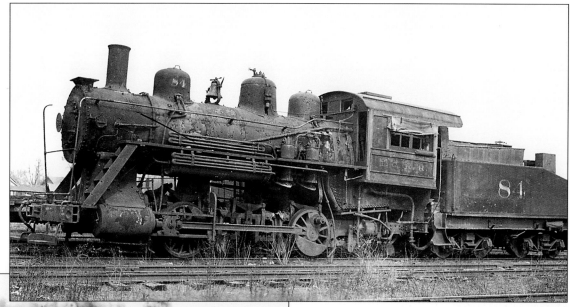

Illinois Central Locomotive #1012 Type 4-4-2 Atlantic. Locomotive #1012 was built by Rogers Locomotive Works as #6115 in February 1904 and was retired in March 1941. *Author's Collection.*

Illinois Central Locomotive #1016 Type 4-4-2 Atlantic. Possibly photographed by Robert F. Hanft in Peoria, Illinois, on July 21, 1934, Locomotive #1016 was built by Rogers Locomotive Works as #6219 in April 1904 and was retired in March 1941. *Mike Gruber Collection.*

Illinois Central Locomotive #1018 Type 4-4-2 Atlantic. Photographed at Freeport, Illinois, #1018 was built by Rogers Locomotive Works as #6206 in April 1904. It was renumbered as #2001 in July 1942 and was dropped from the roster by 1947. This was an "improved" locomotive with raised boiler pressure, new cylinder and tender trucks. These Atlantic branch-line rebuilds were not successful! *Author's Collection.*

Illinois Central Locomotive #769 Type 2-8-0 Consolidation. Locomotive #769 was built by Rogers Locomotive Works as #6183 in April 1904. It was scrapped in 1955. *Author's Collection.*

Illinois Central Locomotive #87 Type 0-6-0 Switcher. Locomotive #87 was built by Rogers Locomotive Works as #6212 in July 1904. It was scrapped in June 1934. These Locomotives are on the scrap line. *Author's Collection.*

Illinois Central Locomotive #1025 Type 4-4-2 Atlantic. Photographed on the passenger turntable in Memphis, Tennessee, on June 10, 1907. Locomotive #1025 was built by Rogers Locomotive Works as #6236 in August 1904 and was retired in November 1939. This photo shows locomotive in its "as built" look. Note tender trucks and tailing truck cylinders. *Author's Collection.*

Illinois Central Locomotive #1031 Type 4-6-2 Pacific. Locomotive #1031 was built by Alco Schenectady Locomotive Works as #29542 in November 1905. It was renumbered as #1003 in circa 1942-1943 until its demise on the scrap line in 1952. *Author's Collection.*

Illinois Central Locomotive #854 Type 2-8-0 Consolidation. Locomotive #854 was built by Alco Brooks Locomotive Works as #40365 in July 1906 and was scrapped in 1949. *Author's Collection.*

This 0-6-0 Pacific locomotive belonged to the Illinois Central at one time but its history is unknown. The number shown (#2062) is not an Illinois Central number. At some point it was a conversion to 61-inch drive wheels and used in local and branch-line service. *Author's Collection.*

Illinois Central Locomotive #942 Type 2-8-0 Consolidation. Photographed in Birmingham, Alabama, in September 1935, #942 was built by Baldwin Locomotive Works as #33740 in September 1909. It was renumbered as #856 in 1943 and was retired in January 1946. *Author's Collection.*

Illinois Central Locomotive #904 Type 2-8-0 Consolidation. Built by Baldwin Locomotive Works as #36149 in February 1911, and photographed in Evansville, Indiana, in 1947 by J.B. Allen, it began its life as IC #983 and was one of 12 original 900 series locomotives modernized by Paducah Shops. It was scrapped in 1952. *Author's Collection.*

Illinois Central Locomotive #906 Type 2-8-0 Consolidation. Photographed in Bloomington, Illinois, on May 28, 1955, by Charles T. Felstead (bottom photograph). (Top photograph taken in Kankakee, Illinois.) Locomotive #906 was built by Baldwin Locomotive Works as #36159 in February 1911. It was originally numbered as #989 and renumbered to #906 in 1943, and was scrapped or sold in July 1955. *Mike Gruber Collection.*

Illinois Central Locomotive #966 Type 2-8-0 Consolidation. Locomotive #966 was built by Baldwin Locomotive Works as #36078 in February 1911. It was improved and renumbered in 1943 along with 11 others. This one kept its original cylinders and worked on the Cedar Rapids, Iowa Divisions Dubuque District until the Iowa Division "dieselized" in 1955. It finished its career working on the Bloomington, Illinois, branch. These engines were originally delivered with Vanderbilt tenders, though many were swapped with other engines when the IC engine-rebuilding program began in 1937. Scrapped in November 1955. *Author's Collection.*

Illinois Central Locomotive #907 Type 2-8-0 Consolidation. Photographed by Paul Stringham in Bloomington, Illinois, on December 5, 1955. Locomotive #907 was built by Baldwin Locomotive Works as #36180 in March 1911. It was originally numbered as #993 and renumbered to #907 in 1943, and was scrapped or sold in July 1956. *Mike Gruber Collection.*

Illinois Central Locomotive #991 Type 2-8-0 Consolidation. Locomotive #991 was built by Baldwin Locomotive Works as #36179 in March 1911. It was sold to Merced & Big River in September 1939 and remained in service there as #991. *Author's Collection.*

Illinois Central Locomotive #1634 Type 2-8-2 Mikado. Locomotive #1634 was built by Baldwin Locomotive Works as #36760 in July 1911. It was rebuilt in November 1942 into a Type 0-8-2 Switcher and renumbered as #3690. Locomotive #3690 was sold in 1955 to B & ZC Company. *Author's Collection.*

Illinois Central Locomotive #2135 Type 2-8-2 Mikado. Locomotive #2135 was built by Baldwin Locomotive Works as #36651 in July 1911. It was originally numbered as #1616 then rebuilt as a hybrid Mikado and renumbered as #2135 in July 1942. It was scrapped in January 1957. All 40 in this class seemed to be different, but as a class they were considered to be the IC's most powerful locomotives. *Mike Gruber Collection.*

Illinois Central Locomotive #1683 Type 2-8-2 Mikado. Locomotive #1683 was built by Baldwin Locomotive Works as #37463 in January 1912. It was retired in March 1941. *Author's Collection.*

Illinois Central Locomotive #2116 Type 2-8-2 Mikado. Photographed in Peoria, Illinois, on May 30, 1948, #2116 was built by Baldwin Locomotive Works as #37465 in January 1912. It was originally numbered as #1685 and rebuilt in February 1939, using a combination of a Mikado boiler with a cut down central-type frame and cylinders, and then renumbered to #2116 and scrapped in May 1955. *Mike Gruber Collection.*

Illinois Central Locomotive #2087 Type 4-6-2 Pacific. Locomotive #2087 was built by Alco Brooks Locomotive Works as #52147 in October 1912. It was originally numbered as #1098 and renumbered to #2087. This is an example of a Paducah, Kentucky Shops rebuild into a branch-line Pacific. These rebuilds of elderly Pacific's were very successful and well regarded by the crews. It was scrapped in August 1947. *Author's Collection.*

Illinois Central Locomotive #1598 Type 2-8-2 Mikado. Locomotive #1598 was built by Baldwin Locomotive Works as #38857 in November 1912. This is one of two examples of IC Mikados with Elesco feedwater heaters. It was retired in March 1941. *Author's Collection.*

Illinois Central Locomotive #1600 Type 2-8-2 Mikado. Photographed on September 22, 1936, #1600 was built by Baldwin Locomotive Works as #38859 in November 1912. It was rebuilt in September 1941 to 2-8-2 #2121 with the boiler placed on a cut down frame from 2901 class 2-10-2 Central Type, and scrapped in June 1957. *Mike Gruber Collection.*

Illinois Central Locomotive #233 Type 0-6-0 Six-Wheel Switcher. Locomotive #233 photographed in Centralia, Illinois, in September 1940 was built by the Alco Pittsburgh Works as #53179 in February 1913, and was dropped from the roster in 1951. *Mike Gruber Collection.*

Illinois Central Locomotive #238 Type 0-6-0 Six-Wheel Switcher. Locomotive #238 was built by the Alco Pittsburgh Works as #53184 in February 1913 and was scrapped in 1952. *Author's Collection.*

Illinois Central Locomotive #1505 Type 2-8-2 Mikado. Locomotive #1505 was built by Baldwin Locomotive Works as #41377 in May 1914. It was rebuilt in April 1940 and the boiler placed on former locomotive #2959 of the 2901 class 2-10-2 Central type chassis without trailing trucks to create 2-10-0 Decapod #3619, which was scrapped in August 1957. *Author's Collection.*

Illinois Central Locomotive #250 Type 0-6-0 Six-Wheel Switcher engine photographed in Baton Rouge, Louisiana, on March 23, 1948. Locomotive #250 was built by Alco Schenectady Works as #54736 in June 1914 and was scrapped in 1953. *Mike Gruber Collection.*

Illinois Central Locomotive #252 Type 0-6-0 Six-Wheel Switcher. Locomotive #252 was built by Alco Schenectady Works as #54738 in June 1914 and was scrapped in 1953. *Mike Gruber Collection.*

Illinois Central Locomotive #1730 Type 2-8-2 Mikado. Photographed by Paul Slager on August 19, 1950, in Markham, Illinois. Locomotive #1730 was built by Lima Locomotive Works as #5034 in May 1915. It was sold or scrapped in May 1955. *Mike Gruber Collection.*

Illinois Central Locomotive #2102 Type 2-8-2 Mikado. Photographed in Freeport, Illinois, #2102 was built by Lima Locomotive Works as #5197 in February 1916. Locomotive #2102 was rebuilt from #1768 in April 1938 and renumbered at that time to #2102. This locomotive shows the initial look of the #2100 class rebuilds that used boilers from 2-8-2s and cut down frames from 2-10-2s. The 2-10-2 boilers were then placed on the #2500 class 4-8-2 rebuilds. Forty locomotives made up this group of hybrid Mikados. It was retired in February 1960. *Author's Collection.*

Illinois Central Locomotive #1141 Type 4-6-2 Pacific. Locomotive #1141 was built by Alco Brooks Locomotive Works as #56085 in October 1916. It was scrapped in 1949. *Author's Collection.*

Illinois Central Locomotive #1146 Type 4-6-2 Pacific was one of the first streamlined Illinois Central locomotives. It was built by Alco Brooks Locomotive Works as #56090 in October 1916. It was the only streamlined steamer clone to replace E-unit diesel on the City of New Orleans connecting train from Louisville to Fulton, Kentucky, train #101-102 in April 1947. Wrecked in 1951, it was scrapped in the field on the Kentucky Cardinal. Painted to fit in with the streamlined cars the locomotive was hated by the crews that had to run it. *Author's Collection.*

Illinois Central Locomotive #307 Type 0-6-0 Six-Wheel Switcher was photographed by Charles T. Felstead in Jackson, Mississippi, on September 14, 1948. Locomotive #307 was built by Alco Cooke Locomotive Works as #58175 in November 1917. It was sold to Crystal Springs S & G Company in June 1952. *Mike Gruber Collection.*

Illinois Central Locomotive #313 Type 0-6-0 Switcher. Locomotive #313 was built by Alco Cooke Locomotive Works as #58181 in November 1917. It was scrapped in April 1954. *Author's Collection.*

Illinois Central Locomotives #1800 and #1806 Type 2-8-2 Mikados. This pair was built by Baldwin Locomotive Works as #48952 and #49353 in June and July 1918. Locomotive #1800 was renumbered to #1288 in February 1938 and was sold or scrapped in May 1955. Locomotive #1806 was renumbered to #1294 in November 1941, renumbered again to #1505 in January 1951 to make room for diesel numbers, and scrapped in February 1956. *Author's Collection.*

Illinois Central Locomotive #1299 Type 2-8-2 Mikado. Photographed in Clinton, Illinois, on October 13, 1952, by Paul Stringham, #1299 was built by Baldwin Locomotive Works as #49641 in August 1918. It was originally numbered as #1811 and renumbered to #1299 in November 1943. It was scrapped in 1955. *Mike Gruber Collection.*

Illinois Central Locomotive #2099 Type 4-6-2 Pacific. Locomotive #2099 was built by Baldwin Locomotive Works as #51199 in February 1919. It was originally numbered by Vicksburg, Shreveport & Pacific as #380. It was renumbered to #1300 in 1926, renumbered again to #994 in July 1937, renumbered to #1000 in May 1943, and scrapped or sold in May 1955. *Author's Collection.*

Illinois Central Locomotive #1198 Type 4-6-2 Pacific. Photographed in Clinton, Illinois, on July 24, 1947, by Paul Stringham. Locomotive #1198 was built by Alco Schenectady Locomotive Works as #62535 in October 1920 and scrapped in 1952. *Mike Gruber Collection.*

Illinois Central Locomotive #1136 Type 4-6-2 Pacific. Locomotive #1136 was built by Alco Schenectady as #62538 in October 1920. Locomotive #1136 was originally numbered as #1201 and received Paducah Shops improvements, including disc main driver, air pumps moved to pilot mounting, and the tender reworked for more water capacity. It was renumbered to #1028 in 1937 and scrapped in February 1953. *Author's Collection.*

Illinois Central Locomotive #2528 Type 4-8-2 Mountain locomotive. Locomotive #2528 was originally built by Lima Locomotive Works in February 1921 as a 2-10-2 and rebuilt in August 1939 with a new cast frame. Photographed by R. J. Foster, #2528 was retired from the roster in October 1960. *Mike Gruber Collection.*

Illinois Central Locomotive #2530 Type 4-8-2 Mountain locomotive. Photographed in East St. Louis, Illinois, on August 23, 1949. Locomotive #2530 was originally built in February 1921 by Lima Locomotive Works as a 2-10-2 and rebuilt to a 4-8-2 in September 1939. It was retired from the roster in October 1956. *Mike Gruber Collection.*

Illinois Central Locomotive #2524 Type 4-8-2 Mountain locomotive. Photographed by R. J. Foster, #2524 was built by Lima Locomotive Works as #6166, a 2-10-2 Type locomotive #2935 in May 1921. It was rebuilt with a new cast frame in May 1939, renumbered as #2524, and dropped from the roster between 1960 and 1962. *Mike Gruber Collection.*

Illinois Central Locomotive #2526 Type 4-8-2 Mountain locomotive. Photographed by R. J. Foster, #2526 was built by Lima Locomotive Works as #6199 in May 1921 as a 2-10-2 locomotive. It was originally numbered as #2962 and renumbered again to #3612, then finally to #2526. It was rebuilt in September 1939 to a Type 4-8-2 Mountain locomotive. It was scrapped in October 1956. *Mike Gruber Collection.*

Illinois Central Locomotive #3507 Type 0-8-0 Eight-Wheel Switcher. Locomotive #3507 was built by Baldwin Locomotive Works as #54803 in May 1921. It was retired in December 1959. *Mike Gruber Collection.*

Illinois Central Locomotive #3512 Type 0-8-0 Eight-Wheel Switcher. Locomotive #3512 was built by Baldwin Locomotive Works as #54812 in May 1921. Photographed in Freeport, Illinois, #3512 was scrapped in 1960 after serving the Illinois Central Railroad for 39 years. *Author's Collection.*

Illinois Central Locomotive #2802 Type 2-10-2 Central. Photographed in Bluford, Illinois, by R.J. Foster on June 17, 1956, #2802 was built by Lima Locomotive Works as #6180 in June 1921. It was originally numbered as #2949 and renumbered to #2802 in July 1944. Between December 1943 and December 1945, all locomotives between #2019-2081 were modernized with new boilers identical to the Paducah-built 4-8-2 Mountain locomotives creating, quite arguably, American railroading's most powerful 2-10-2s intended to move meat trains over the Iowa Divisions Dubuque District between Waterloo, Iowa, and Freeport, Illinois. Locomotive #2802 was dropped from the roster between 1960 and 1962. *Mike Gruber Collection.*

Illinois Central Locomotive #2536 Type 4-8-2 Mountain locomotive. Photographed by R. J. Foster, #2536 was originally built by Lima Locomotive Works in July 1921 as a 2-10-2 and rebuilt with a cast frame in March 1940. It was retired from the roster in January 1959. *Mike Gruber Collection.*

Illinois Central Locomotive #2711 Type 2-10-2 Central. Locomotive #2711 was built by Lima Locomotive Works as #6214 in July 1921. It was originally numbered as #2977 and renumbered to #2711 in May 1943. It was retired in October 1960. *Author's Collection.*

Illinois Central Locomotive #2720 Type 2-10-2 Central. Photographed in East St. Louis, Illinois, on September 8, 1945. Locomotive #3720 was built by Lima Locomotive Works as #6222 in July 1921. It was originally numbered as #2985 and renumbered to #2720 in August 1943. It was retired in December 1959. *Mike Gruber Collection.*

Illinois Central Locomotive #2728 Type 2-10-2 Central. Photographed in East St. Louis, Illinois, on September 20, 1945. Locomotive #2728 was built by Lima Locomotive Works as #6231 in July 1921. It was originally numbered as #2994 and was "modernized" and renumbered to #2728 in November 1943. It was retired from the roster between 1960 and 1962. *Mike Gruber Collection.*

Illinois Central Locomotive #2745 Type 2-10-2 Central. Photographed in East St. Louis, Illinois, on June 7, 1953. Locomotive #2745 was built by Lima Locomotive Works as #6210 in July 1921. It was originally numbered as #2973 and renumbered to #2745 in May 1944. It was retired in December 1959. *Mike Gruber Collection.*

Illinois Central Locomotive #2964 Type 2-10-2 Central. Locomotive #2964 was built by Lima Locomotive Works as #6221 in July 1921. It was renumbered as #2700 in January 1943, and scrapped in 1955. *Author's Collection.*

Illinois Central Locomotive #2735 Type 2-10-2 Central. Photographed in Wamac, Illinois, in April 1946, #2735 was built by Lima Locomotive Works as #6237 in August 1921. It was originally numbered as #3000 and renumbered to #2735 in February 1944. It was scrapped in October 1956. *Mike Gruber Collection.*

Illinois Central Locomotive #2741 Type 2-10-2 Central. Photographed in Bluford, Illinois, on September 2, 1956, #2741 was built by Lima Locomotive Works as #6227 in August 1921. It was originally numbered as #2990 and renumbered to #2741 in April 1944. It was retired in October 1960. *Mike Gruber Collection.*

Illinois Central Locomotive #2743 Type 2-10-2 Central. Photographed in Centralia, Illinois, in June 1956, #2743 was built by Lima Locomotive Works as #6228 in August 1921. It was originally numbered as #2991 and renumbered to #2743 in April 1944. It was scrapped in December 1956. *Mike Gruber Collection.*

Illinois Central Locomotive #2538 Type 4-8-2 Mountain locomotive. Photographed in Markham, Illinois, #2538 was originally built by Lima Locomotive Works as a 2-10-2 and rebuilt with a new cast frame in May 1940. Locomotive #2538 was retired from the roster in October 1960. *Mike Gruber Collection.*

Illinois Central Locomotive #2548 Type 4-8-2 Mountain locomotive. Photographed by R. J. Foster on May 12, 1949, #2548 was originally built in 1921 by Lima Locomotive Works as a 2-10-2 and rebuilt with a new cast frame in May 1942. Locomotive #2548 was retired from the roster in October 1960. *Mike Gruber Collection.*

Illinois Central Locomotive #2553 Type 4-8-2 Mountain locomotive. Photographed in Clinton, Illinois, on September 23, 1953, by Paul Stringham, #2553 was originally built by Lima Locomotive Works in 1921 as a 2-10-2 and rebuilt in August 1942. Locomotive #2553 was scrapped in October 1956. *Mike Gruber Collection.*

Illinois Central Locomotive #2817 Type 2-10-2 Central. Locomotive #2817 was built by Lima Locomotive Works. This locomotive was probably built in 1921 or 1922 but roster information is unclear. Locomotives in this series were renumbered to #2800-2819 in the 1940s and given new boilers and placed in a storage fleet for a call back into service that never came. This locomotive was probably scrapped in the very late 1950s. *Author's Collection.*

Illinois Central Locomotive #1002 Type 4-6-2 Pacific. Locomotive #1002 was built by Baldwin Locomotive Works as #55416 in May 1922. It was originally numbered as #480 for the Alabama & Vicksburg Railroad. It was renumbered in 1926 to #1302, renumbered again to #996 in July 1937, and renumbered again to #1002 in May 1943 when it was rebuilt. It was scrapped in May 1955. *Author's Collection.*

Illinois Central Locomotive #3103 Type 2-10-2 was acquired along with locomotives numbered #3100-3104 in 1926 from the Alabama & Vicksburg Railroad. Locomotive #3103 was built by Baldwin Locomotive Works as #55478 in June 1922. It was originally numbered as #473 for the Alabama & Vicksburg Railroad and renumbered in 1926 to #3103. In September 1937 it was rebuilt to a Type 0-10-0 and renumbered to #3605. It was scrapped in 1950. *Author's Collection.*

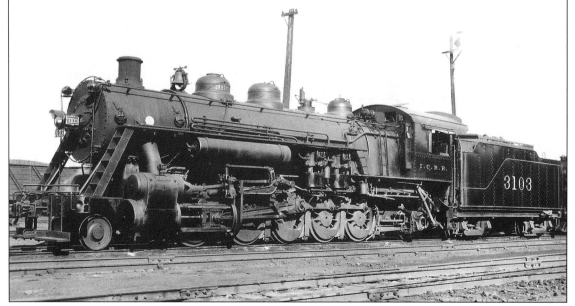

Illinois Central Locomotive #3400 Type 0-10-0 Switcher along with #3401 were built by Baldwin Locomotive Works as #55578 and #57669 in July 1922 and March 1924 and were acquired when the Alabama & Vicksburg Railroad was absorbed into Illinois Central. Both were renumbered to #3600 and #3601 after upgrading at Paducah, Kentucky, shops; these two were the IC's most powerful switchers. *Author's Collection.*

Illinois Central Locomotive #2705 Type 2-10-2 Central. Photographed on July 24, 1949, #2705 was built by Lima Locomotive Works as #6329 in December 1922. It was originally numbered as #3003 and renumbered to #2705 in January 1943. It was scrapped in January 1957. *Mike Gruber Collection.*

Illinois Central Locomotive #1675 Type 2-8-2 Mikado. Locomotive #1675 was built by Alco Schenectady Locomotive Works as #63615 in January 1923. Locomotive #1675 was improved at Paducah Shops in the spring of 1938 and renumbered to #1375 and renumbered again in March 1954 to #1675 to make room for the diesel numbers. It was retired in 1954. Photo appears to have been taken in Paducah, Kentucky. *Author's Collection.*

Illinois Central Locomotive #2537 Type 4-8-2 Mountain locomotive. Photographed by R. J. Foster, #2537 was originally built by Lima Locomotive Works in January 1923 as a 2-10-2 and rebuilt with a cast frame in April 1940. It was scrapped in January 1957. *Mike Gruber Collection.*

Illinois Central Locomotive #2807 Type 1-10-2 Central. Photographed by R. J. Foster, #2807 was built by Lima Locomotive Works as #6339 in January 1923. It was originally numbered as #3013 and renumbered to #2807 in September 1944. It was dropped from the roster between 1960 and 1962. *Mike Gruber Collection.*

Illinois Central Locomotive #1442 Type 2-8-2 Mikado. Locomotive #1442 was built by Lima Locomotive Works as #6546 in October 1923. It was originally numbered as #1954 and was renumbered to #1442 in October 1942. This locomotive was rebuilt in 1941 and was scrapped in January 1957. *Author's Collection.*

Illinois Central Locomotive #2400 Type 4-8-2 Mountain locomotive. Locomotive #2400 was built by Alco Schenectady Locomotive Works as #64569 in October 1923. The 2400 class Mountain locomotives were the premier passenger engines until being replaced by the diesel E-Units. The Illinois Central also recognized early in their career that they were excellent freight engines and quite possibly influenced the IC to convert the Centrals to this wheel arrangement when they began to rebuild the fleet at Paducah, Kentucky, in 1930. The Mountain locomotives were highly regarded by the crews. The IC purchased the fleet of Mountain locomotives in three groups of 20: 20 Lima, 20 Alco, and 20 more Lima. This locomotive was retired in 1960 as diesels took over the IC fleet. *Mike Gruber Collection.*

Illinois Central Locomotive #2401 Type 4-8-2 Mountain locomotive. Photographed in Chicago on July 4, 1941, #2401 was built by Alco Schenectady Locomotive Works as #64570 in October 1923. It was scrapped in January 1957. *Mike Gruber Collection.*

Illinois Central Locomotive #1527 Type 2-8-2 Mikado. Locomotive #1527 was built by Lima Locomotive Works as #6565 in January 1924. It was originally numbered as #1973, renumbered to #1461 in June 1940, renumbered again to #1527 in May 1952, and was retired in February 1960. *Author's Collection.*

Illinois Central Locomotive #2350 Type 4-8-2 Mountain locomotive. Photographed by Charles T. Felstead in Bluford, Illinois, on July 2, 1952, it was built by Lima Locomotive Works as #6884 in December 1924. Originally numbered as #2415, Paducah Shops rebuilt and upgraded this locomotive and her sisters (#2351-#2352) to create a trio from the "Seminole" service. These locomotives were upgraded to the 2400 class for service on trains #9-10 on the "Seminole" between Jackson, Tennessee, and Birmingham, Alabama, to handle the grades encountered on this line. The original tenders were also put back on due to the short Frisco turntable in Birmingham. After diesels took over on the "Seminole" these locomotives were put back into freight service. *Mike Gruber Collection.*

Illinois Central Locomotive #2352 Type 4-8-2 Mountain locomotive. Locomotive #2352 was built by Lima Locomotive Works as #6889 in December 1924. This is the passenger configuration as imposed by a "too short" Frisco turntable. It was originally numbered as #2420 and renumbered to #2352 in 1944-1945. It was scrapped in January 1957. *Author's Collection.*

Illinois Central Locomotive #2422 Type 4-8-2 Mountain locomotive. Locomotive #2422 was built by Alco Schenectady Locomotive Works as #6891 in December 1924. It was scrapped in February 1960. Locomotive #2307 in background is upgraded sister to #2422. *Mike Gruber Collection.*

Illinois Central Locomotive #2425 Type 4-8-2 Mountain locomotive. Photographed in Effingham, Illinois, on October 24, 1939, #2425 was built by Alco Schenectady Locomotive Works as #6894 in December 1924. It was retired from the roster in February 1960. *Mike Gruber Collection.*

Illinois Central Locomotive #7008 Type 2-8-4 Berkshire. Locomotive #7008 was built by Lima Locomotive Works as #7144 in October 1926. Photographed leaving the Century of Progress grounds after being exhibited there, it was renumbered as #8004 in February 1940. It was scrapped or sold in August 1954. *Author's Collection.*

Illinois Central Locomotive #1 Type 4-6-4 Hudson. Locomotive #1 was built by Lima Locomotive Works as #7175 in November 1926. Locomotive #1 was converted from 2-8-4-wheel configuration by IC Paducah Shops to a 4-6-4 for fast merchandise freight service. Locomotive #1 was American railroading's only Hudson built for freight. It was not a success and no more 2-8-4 Limas were converted to this wheel arrangement. It was dropped from the roster between 1945 and 1951. *Author's Collection.*

Illinois Central Locomotive #2440 Type 4-8-2 Mountain locomotive. Locomotive #2440 was built by Alco Schenectady Locomotive Works as #67039 in September 1926. It was retired from the roster in February 1960. *Mike Gruber Collection.*

Illinois Central Locomotive #3553 Type 0-8-0 Eight-Wheel Switcher. Locomotive #3553 was built by Baldwin Locomotive Works as #60126 in July 1927. Photographed in Carbondale, Illinois, on May 3, 1955, #3553 was retired from the roster in February 1960. This was one of the last steam locomotives on the Illinois Central Railroad. *Mike Gruber Collection.*

Illinois Central Locomotive #3558 Type 0-8-0 Switcher. Locomotive #3558 was built by Lima Locomotive Works as #7360 in June 1929. Photographed in the Jackson, Mississippi, yard on September 15, 1941, #3558 survived the wreck and was retired from the roster in February 1960. The other locomotive, #1457 in the wreck, also built by Lima, was scrapped in 1956. *Author's Collection.*

Illinois Central Locomotive #3568 Type 0-8-0 Eight-Wheel Switcher. Photographed in Decatur, Illinois, by Paul Stringham on May 5, 1954, #3568 was built by Lima Locomotive Works as #7370 in June 1929. It was scrapped in August 1957. Notice the engineer breaking a smile for the camera. *Mike Gruber Collection.*

Illinois Central Locomotive #1446 Type 2-6-0 Mogul. Photographed in Wamac, Illinois, in August 1933, #1446 was built by Schenectady Locomotive Works as #2989 in December 1889. It was originally numbered as #453 and was renumbered as #858 in 1890, was renumbered again to #1858 in May 1904, and renumbered again in May 1917 to #2858. It was rebuilt at Burnside Shop into a Type 2-6-4-T in May 1921 for Suburban service and renumbered to #1446. It was scrapped June 1943. *Author's Collection.*

Pretty as can be, this locomotive is dressed up for the 1968 film *Gaily Gaily*. Part of the movie was filmed at the Illinois Central Depot in Galena, Illinois. A number of Galena area residents played parts as extras in the movie. This locomotive never saw service on the Illinois Central Railroad. McLoud Lumber Company owned it for many years. Today this engine is awaiting restoration at the Mid-Continent Railroad Museum in North Freedom, Wisconsin. *Jim Sands Photograph.*

Illinois Central Locomotive #14 McKeen Passenger Train. Photographed in Belleville, Wisconsin, in summer 1908, Locomotive #14 was built by McKeen for the Union Pacific Railroad. This train made several round trips each day from Freeport, Illinois, to Madison, Wisconsin. The theory behind the McKeens was great, one piece of equipment to handle passengers and light freight. Unfortunately they didn't work up to expectations. This section of track was the last remaining Illinois Central track in Wisconsin. It was removed in 1999 after a long battle to save the rails. *Fred Solberger Collection.*

Illinois Central Victory Train at Belleville, Wisconsin, shortly after the conclusion of WWI. Notice the large crowds of people to welcome this train to the small village. A tank similar to the one on the flatcar was taken off the car and driven around the streets of Belleville while the train was at the depot. This depot, built in 1888, is still standing. *Photos courtesy Jerry Remy/ Belleville Historical Society.*

No book on railroads would be complete without a train wreck photograph. The location of this one is uncertain but appears to have been somewhere in Iowa, perhaps near Dubuque. The only information on the photograph is, "Wreck in which Matt Clancy was killed." *Author's Collection.*

Single for *Flexibility*

Double for **POWER**

Scores of new diesel switchers like these move freight swiftly through Illinois Central yards. Used together as a single operating unit, two of these diesels deliver 2400 horsepower. Used apart, they can be doing important work in two places at the same time. Which means better service for Illinois Central shippers everywhere.

Illinois Central Railroad

Main Line of Mid-America

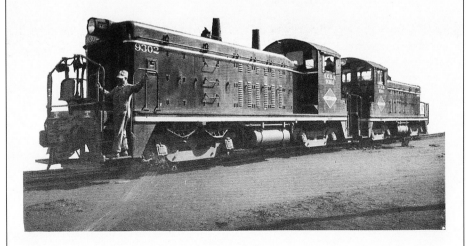

November 5, 1951   RAILWAY AGE

Diesel advertisement. *Author's Collection.*

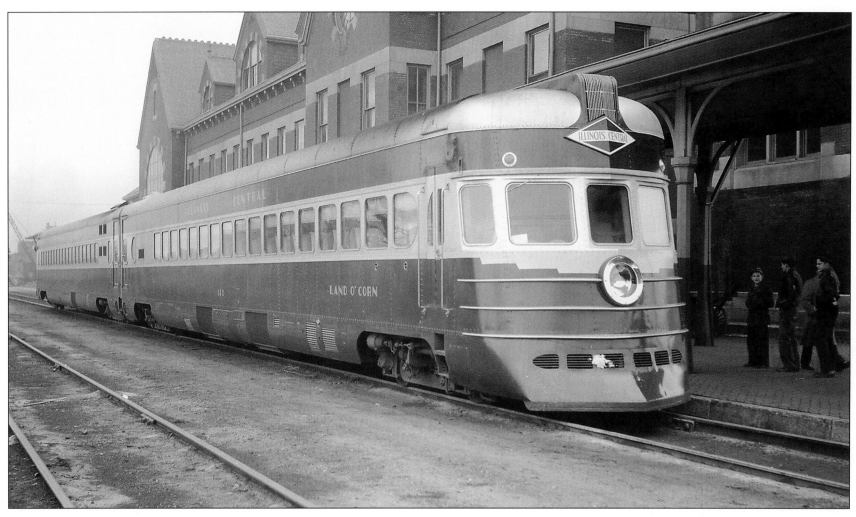

"The Land O' Corn," Illinois Central Diesel Motor Car #140/141 photographed at Dubuque, Iowa, on October 3, 1940. This locomotive set was built by American Car & Foundry in 1940. It was powered by two 450-horsepower engines. Wrecked on February 18, 1942, it was sold to New York, Sesquehanna & Western Railroad in 1943 where it was renumbered to #1005-06. Photographed by Duane Bearse at eastbound #14 from Waterloo, Iowa, to Chicago. *Mike Gruber Collection.*

The Green Diamond photographed in Decatur, Illinois, on May 4, 1936. EMC/St. Louis Car Company built this beauty. The Green Diamond is on display while touring the Midwest prior to being placed in regular service. It was pulled from Green Diamond service from Chicago to St. Louis in 1947 and replaced with an E-Unit and lightweight streamlined equipment. Serious consideration was given to using this articulated trainset in Chicago to Waterloo, Iowa, as Land O' Corn service. This plan was rejected and the trainset was sent south to operate as the "Miss Lou" between Jackson, Mississippi and New Orleans, Louisanna. Due to frequent breakdowns it was scrapped in 1950. *Mike Gruber Collection.*

Another photograph of the Green Diamond on the move at Relay Junction, East St. Louis, Illinois. The Green Diamond premiered on the Illinois Central Railroad in March 1936. The Illinois Central sent this train on a 7,500-mile goodwill exhibition trip across the Illinois Central system. By the conclusion of the trip over 414,000 people had gone through the train. *Mike Gruber Collection.*

After the Green Diamond tour was completed the train went into scheduled passenger service between Chicago and St. Louis. On May 17, 1936, the new Green Diamond service was christened in Chicago. The christening ceremony was held system wide. *Mike Gruber Collection.*

City of Miami advertisement. *Author's Collection.*

119

Original *City of Miami* passenger train. General Motors EMD (Electromotive Division) built this E-6 #4000. This locomotive was wrecked in May 1947 and traded in for E-7 #4000. *Mike Gruber Collection.*

City of Miami. A seven-car diesel-powered streamliner, the *City of Miami* was placed in service on December 18, 1940. The train made a round trip every third day. At this time the Illinois Central had spent $3 million to purchase seven new streamlined passenger trains. *Mike Gruber Collection.*

City of Miami. The Illinois Central actively promoted tourism via its trains. As an inducement to use their passenger trains Illinois Central added a second streamliner in the winter of 1951-1952 enabling passengers to get a train to Miami two out of three days instead of the every third day service that was previously available. *Mike Gruber Collection.*

Illinois Central EMD E-7 Locomotive #4006 photographed by Duane Bearse in Dubuque, Iowa, on February 13, 1947. This is the inaugural run of the eastbound #14 conventional streamlined Land O' Corn. Locomotive #4006 was often seen on the head end of the *City of New Orleans* passenger trains. Locomotive #4006 was built in September 1946 and retired in May 1969 in a trade to Precision Engineering for five ex-Florida East Coast E-9As. *Mike Gruber Collection.*

A meeting near Amite, Louisiana, on May 29, 1962 of what would be Illinois Central's freight and passenger power for almost two decades. General Purpose GP 7&9 models for freight in all-black trimmed in white striping and numbers. The Green Diamond proudly emblazoned with white on the side of the cab. All EMD E-Unit models 6, 7, 8, and 9 wore Panama colors. *Mike Gruber Collection.*

Splendor in the night. This group of five Illinois Central freight trains at the Chicago terminal is standing ready to pull out when given the signal. The center train is the MS-1, the fastest freight train in the world at the time. The MS-1 could travel the 527-mile route to Memphis in 13 hours and 5 minutes. Other trains are destined for Sioux City, St. Louis, Cincinnati and Birmingham.

A Word from the Author

April 1979: It's well past dark and the boys are fast asleep in their beds. Low clouds hide the nearly full moon. A typical April night, slight warmth to the breeze, the smell of burning grass and leaves fill the air. This is one of those nights when a walk on the old railroad bed is in order.

A short, two-minute walk gets me to the abandoned Milwaukee Road right-of-way. I head toward Monticello as I always do when I walk at night in early spring. My grandfather and I made this same walk numerous times nearly three decades earlier. The first spring peepers of the season fill the air with their music. Creosote odors from the bridge timbers linger long after the train has left town for the last time. The clouds open for a minute to reveal a beautiful moon that will be full in two nights.

The walking is easy. Each step is savored. I pause to listen once more to the spring peepers. Then I hear a faint sound to the east. Not sure what it is, I continue on until I hear the sound again. Can it be the Illinois Central heading north to Madison?

I listen more intently now trying to pinpoint the sound I hear. Again, the same sound penetrates the April air, a sound I recall from years earlier. I listen and again hear the train whistle. Each time it gets a bit louder. Then my grandfather's words come back to me.

"If you hear the Illinois Central train pulling the grade to the tunnel you can expect rain or snow within 24 hours." Those words came back with such force I stopped to ponder the meaning of the distant sound.

There was some far deeper meaning than just a train whistle in the distance. I stood silently thinking of what to make of this. I recalled reading a story some years earlier of a farmer in Lincoln County, Wisconsin. Taking his children outside on a cold February night in 1957 they heard the mournful sound of the last Wisconsin timber wolf howling in the night.

Little did I know at the time that the mournful Illinois Central train whistle I was listening to was telling the same story as the wolf. The story of being the last of its species in Wisconsin. Extirpation would soon follow.

Several years later a passenger special was scheduled to run from Monroe to Belleville, Wisconsin. My boys and I got up early that morning and hurried to the nearest crossing. We walked the right-of-way to the Stewart Tunnel to await the arrival of the train.

We waited for what seemed to be an eternity. And our wait was worth it. The stillness of the day was broken with the diesel horn blowing for the south portal of the tunnel. Within a couple of minutes huge clouds of fog billowed out of the north portal signaling the train's exit from the tunnel. The boys stood in awe of this thing of beauty as it emerged.

In early May 1999, after the decision had been made to remove the Illinois Central rails from Monroe to Madison, Wisconsin, I received a call from a friend. He asked if I wanted to join him and a couple of his friends to take what ended up being the last trip of a railroad vehicle on the former Illinois Central line.

My oldest son, Terry, joined us in offering our tearful farewell to an old friend. Somehow it seems that one can't get emotionally involved with iron and wood, but it happens. The day was picture perfect. Under other circumstances this would have been a fun trip. Unfortunately we knew that we would be the last people to ever ride the last remaining Illinois Central rails in Wisconsin. We trespassed with our motorcar but we had to get to a funeral that Sunday morning. The cemetery where the funeral was to be held was the 100-foot wide Illinois Central right-of-way that was our history.

Sadness fills me. My sons will never have the chance to teach their children to listen for the train whistle in the distant night. Grandpa was correct. It rained within 24 hours of the last time I heard the Illinois Central whistle.

KDT—August 2001

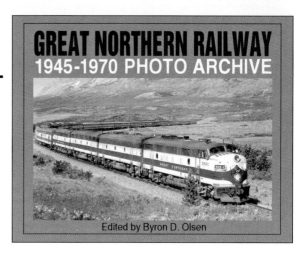
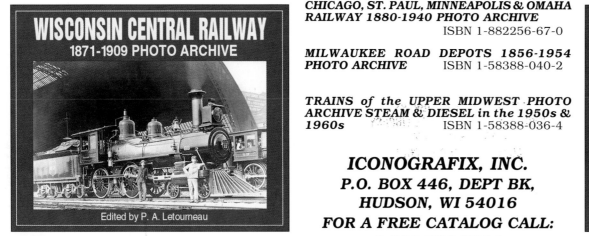
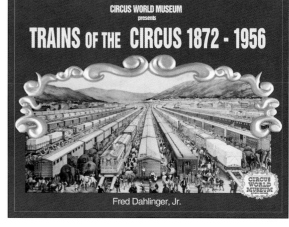

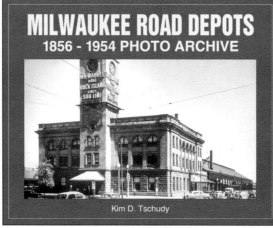
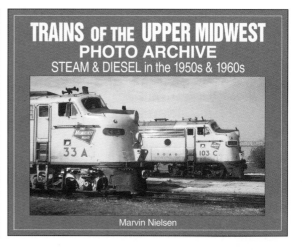